When You Have an Unsaved Loved One

52 Devotions to Give You Hope

Mary Stone

Disclaimer: This book is not intended as a stand-in for counseling or therapy. The verses and subsequent messages are intended to encourage, enlighten, and help you grow individually and relationally with your unsaved loved one. The Holy Spirit is the one true Counselor who seeks to speak to you and your beloved.

When You Have an Unsaved Loved One

Also by Mary Stone

Non-Fiction

Run in the Path of Peace—the Secret of Being Content No Matter What

When Your Wife Gets on Your Nerves—or Worse; 52 Verses to Bolster You

When Your Husband is a Christian—But Doesn't Always Act Like One; 52 Verses to Lift You Up

Fiction

In BeTWEEN TROUBLE

Acknowledgements

I wish to extend a bouquet of appreciation to my dear sister in Christ, Lindy, for providing inspiration and insight as I embarked on writing *When You Have an Unsaved Loved One*.

My immeasurable gratitude goes to our Sovereign God for His Word, His leading, His love, His forgiveness, and His encouragement. Thank You, Lord Jesus, with all my heart!

Table of Contents

When You Have an Unsaved Loved One

52 Devotions to Give You Hope

Why 52 devotions?

When you focus on one verse throughout the week, every week of the year, you store this verse in your mind and heart. By repeating, you go deep within scripture, mining the treasure God has for you in that portion of His Word.

The result? You will be encouraged, strengthened, and armed to intercede for your loved one.

These devotions mention a spouse, a family member, or friend, and might not in each case apply to your situation. But as you memorize the week's verse, ask God what He wants you to come away with for *your* spiritual growth. For these devotions are to equip *you* to never be lacking in zeal, but to keep your spiritual fervor in serving the Lord. And, so you will be joyful in hope, patient in affliction, faithful in prayer. (Romans 12:11-12)

You can be assured, the LORD hears when you call to him. (Psalm 4:3)

~ Week 1 ~

"Thanks be to God, who in Christ always leads us in triumphal procession, and through us spreads the fragrance of the knowledge of Him everywhere."
2 Corinthians 2:14 (ESV)

What great news this is!

This means that as you go through your daily routines and are around those who don't know Jesus as their Lord and Savior, God is at that very moment—through you—spreading the fresh and pleasing fragrance of the knowledge of Him.

Can you imagine this sweet aroma wafting in your wake as you move about? Go a step further and visualize this bouquet enveloping you and your loved ones.

This definitely puts things into a different perspective, don't you think?

Satan would rather have you see your situation as a dark cloud of doom, and in fact, some days that may be what you feel you are in the midst of spiritually when others reject your witness. The next time that cloud descends, rebuke it and replace it with an image of Christ leading you in a triumphal procession, totally enveloped by a delightful fragrance of the knowledge of Him all around you.

How might you cultivate this triumphal procession through a garden of pleasing scent?

~ Week 1 Reflections ~

Day 1   This week's verse in full, or portion thereof:

____

____

____

Day 2   This verse is meaningful to me in that:

____

____

____

Day 3   This verse empowers me to:

____

____

____

Day 4   My response to the question at the end of the devotion:

____

____

____

Day 5   Prayer:

____

____

____

~ **Week 2** ~

"Be patient then, brothers and sisters, until the Lord's coming.
See how the farmer waits for the land to yield its valuable crop,
patiently waiting for the autumn and spring rains."
James 5:7

You plant words, sowing seeds for salvation. You water, wait and watch. Moisture comes and you see sprouts beginning to form. What a delightful sight! All your efforts and prayers are paying off. You get excited for your loved one and the blessings awaiting her/his life in Christ.

But then, drought sets in. Something has happened in this person's life to not only stop but lop off the growth you had seen. The sprigs of faith within your special person wither and disappear before your eyes. (S)he may even withdraw from you, and turn her/his back on the Lord.

Then God draws you near and whispers His promise of 1 Corinthians 15:58: *"Therefore, my dear brothers and sisters, stand firm. Let nothing move you. Always give yourselves fully to the work of the Lord, because you know that your labor in the Lord is not in vain."*

In other words, do not concern yourself with what will happen to your efforts in the end because God's got this!

Even with that said, perhaps patience has never been your virtue. This is a perfect time for you to use impatience as currency. Offer it up to the Lord to trade in for faith.

What valuable and fruitful crops can you see you and your beloved reaping after all?

~ *Week 2 Reflections* ~

Day 1   This week's verse in full, or portion thereof:

____

____

____

Day 2   This verse is meaningful to me in that:

____

____

____

Day 3   This verse empowers me to:

____

____

____

Day 4   My response to the question at the end of the devotion:

____

____

____

Day 5   Prayer:

____

____

____

~ Week 3 ~

"This is what the LORD *says: 'Restrain your voice from weeping and your eyes from tears, for your work will be rewarded,' declares the* LORD*. 'They will return from the land of the enemy. So there is hope for your descendants,' declares the* LORD*."*
Jeremiah 31:16-17

Do waterworks flow from your eyes—tracking tears down your cheeks—over the unsaved condition of your family members? Do wails of weeping burst from your mouth? Such are the circumstances of which this verse in Jeremiah speaks. This is a time-worn situation, but the good news is, throughout the years God has been present and ever faithful to listen and attend to these cries for help.

Is it your child or children you fervently lift to the Lord for His saving grace? If so, this verse can't be clearer . . . "there is hope for your descendants."

God wants you to embrace this hope. Envision what embracing hope looks like. Clutch hope to your heart. Embed it in your mind. Establish it in your spirit. Cling to it without doubt. In other words, when uncertainty or skepticism creeps in, rebuke these spirits of misgivings in the name of Jesus. Ask Him to replace them with a Spirit of faith (2 Corinthians 4:13).

What loved ones' names do you lift up today, claiming the promise of Jeremiah 31:16-17?

~ Week 3 Reflections ~

Day 1   This week's verse in full, or portion thereof:

____

____

____

Day 2   This verse is meaningful to me in that:

____

____

____

Day 3   This verse empowers me to:

____

____

____

Day 4   My response to the question at the end of the devotion:

____

____

____

Day 5   Prayer:

____

____

____

~ **Week 4** ~

"... so is my word that goes out from my mouth: It will not return to me empty, but will accomplish what I desire and achieve the purpose for which I sent it."

Isaiah 55:11

Have you received God's assurance of your loved one's salvation? Yet with each passing year you see no evidence of this? Doubt in the face of God's promise is an age-old struggle.

Abram was 75 years old when God first promised him and Sarai a child. Year after year went by. Four times in all, God spoke this pledge to them. Without evidence of the Lord's vow, doubts assailed them. Not until a quarter of a century later was Isaac born.

The Bible is full of God's promises. You needn't doubt He will bring them about, as His timing is not your timing. Even though you know God keeps His Word, still, you need His help in waiting for things to come to fruition.

This period of anticipation is ripe for deepening your faith. Thanking God for this delay will help you let go of your timeline of expectations. It will help you trust in the Lord to accomplish what He desires and to achieve His purpose.

As you trust God with all your heart, do not rely on your own understanding. For then you will know the Lord is keeping you on the right path of praying and witnessing to your loved one.

Will you thank God now for this wait?

~ *Week 4 Reflections* ~

Day 1   This week's verse in full, or portion thereof:

____

____

____

Day 2   This verse is meaningful to me in that:

____

____

____

Day 3   This verse empowers me to:

____

____

____

Day 4   My response to the question at the end of the devotion:

____

____

____

Day 5   Prayer:

____

____

____

~ Week 5 ~

"I will remember the deeds of the LORD; yes, I will remember your miracles of long ago. I will consider all your works, and meditate on your mighty deeds."
Psalm 77:11-12

It was a time of great need, and in it God's people desperately needed to hear from Him amid the Almighty's silence.

Although Asaph poured out his disappointment and despair in Psalm 77, he began the psalm acknowledging God's presence and character.

Who was Asaph? Chronicles refers to him as one of the three Levites appointed by David to be in charge of singing in the house of Yahweh. Did Asaph sing for joy or were his songs ones of lament?

When you desperately need to hear from the Lord, do you feel like singing?

G. Campbell Morgan writes: "The message of this psalm is that to brood on sorrow is to be broken and disheartened, while to see God is to sing on the darkest day. Once we come to know that our years are of His right hand, there is light everywhere."

David Guzik entitled Psalm 77 "The Troubled Heart Remembers God's Great Works."

Is your heart troubled? If so, ponder on the works of old and the work God has done in your life. Meditate on these things to bring you into your Heavenly Father's presence so you can lift your voice and heart in song. His light will penetrate your darkness.

What song(s) of praise and worship will you sing this moment and throughout the day and week?

~ Week 5 Reflections ~

Day 1   This week's verse in full, or portion thereof:

____

____

____

Day 2   This verse is meaningful to me in that:

____

____

____

Day 3   This verse empowers me to:

____

____

____

Day 4   My response to the question at the end of the devotion:

____

____

____

Day 5   Prayer:

____

____

____

~ **Week 6** ~

"For we live by faith, not by sight."
2 Corinthians 5:7

As you move through your daily routine, what do you observe your loved one doing that disproves a faith in God? Do you count this as proof of her/him falling into the "unsaved" category? Does it seem evidentiary that the Lord has not heard your prayers—or if He has, that He simply isn't answering your heartfelt petitions?

Living by sight can lead to false assumptions. These suppositions can take root and cause you no end to despair and usher you to a dark place mentally and spiritually.

1 Samuel 17:16 reveals that when Saul and all of Israel heard Goliath's boasts, they were dismayed and fearful. But when shepherd boy, David, showed up at the battle and was met by the Philistine's taunts, and he saw the men of Israel flee in terror, David—after meeting with King Saul—returned to the field. Why would he put himself in harm's way?

Living by faith, not by sight, David told Goliath, ". . . for the battle is the LORD's and he will give all of you into our hands." (1 Samuel 17:47)

Take heart and encouragement from David. When you see your loved one refusing to yield to Christ's invitation, refuse to yield to sight. Claim the promise that this battle is the Lord's, and He will deliver the person you love dearly into His hands.

Will you ask Jesus to shine His light all around you so you can see clearly to live by faith?

~ *Week 6 Reflections* ~

Day 1 This week's verse in full, or portion thereof:

____

____

____

Day 2 This verse is meaningful to me in that:

____

____

____

Day 3 This verse empowers me to:

____

____

____

Day 4 My response to the question at the end of the devotion:

____

____

____

Day 5 Prayer:

____

____

____

~ Week 7 ~

"Light in a messenger's eyes brings joy to the heart, and good news gives health to the bones."
Proverbs 15:30

Does light shine in your eyes when you witness? If so, know that it brings joy to your loved one, even if you don't see this evidence at the moment. Further, the good news of God's Word will bring health to her/his bones.

What does it mean when God speaks of giving health to the bones? Is this a promise of physical healing? It certainly could be. However, perhaps our Father is referring to spiritual healing, where your loved one is in need of an internal curative, therapeutic ministration only possible in the spiritual realm.

Has your loved one been deeply wounded, emotionally and or spiritually? If so, God knows all about it and desires to bring wholeness to her/him. The Lord knows what it will take to do this, and is using you as a part of His plan. How exciting is this?

However, God in His infinite wisdom may not share His detailed strategy with you—a good thing, because we are known for getting in God's way, or at best trying to "help" Him out by taking things into our own hands, perhaps to hurry things along.

How can you let your light shine—light which reflects your trust in God and His love for you and your loved one?

~ *Week 7 Reflections* ~

Day 1   This week's verse in full, or portion thereof:

____

____

____

Day 2   This verse is meaningful to me in that:

____

____

____

Day 3   This verse empowers me to:

____

____

____

Day 4   My response to the question at the end of the devotion:

____

____

____

Day 5   Prayer:

____

____

____

~ Week 8 ~

"Be kind and compassionate to one another, forgiving each other, just as in Christ God forgave you."
Ephesians 4:32

Did your husband profess a faith in God when he courted you, and you thought *this is the one*? Especially if number one on your "husband material" list was a commitment to Christ. After you married, did he accompany you to church and say all the right things—only to drift away from God and church activities? And now you wonder if he was saved in the first place?

If so, do you feel betrayed? You had placed your hope for a godly marriage in your faith basket, only to now find it empty of this vital component in the relationship.

Consider David, who in anguish over his love for one close to him whom he trusted, wrote in Psalm 55:12-14: "If an enemy were insulting me, I could endure it; if a foe were rising against me, I could hide. But it is you, a man like myself, my companion, my close friend, with whom I once enjoyed sweet fellowship at the house of God, as we walked about among the worshipers."

Betrayal blasts a short path to not only deep hurt but to distrust as well.

To get beyond this betrayal you must forgive. Forgiveness is an integral part of your spiritual growth. There is no greater example of how to deal with betrayal than Jesus. Judas betrayed Him. Peter betrayed Him. Jesus forgave them with a deep love.

Will you move forward into forgiveness and steadfastness in Christ?

Will you move forward into forgiveness and steadfastness in Christ?

~ Week 8 Reflections ~

Day 1   This week's verse in full, or portion thereof:

____

____

____

Day 2   This verse is meaningful to me in that:

____

____

____

Day 3   This verse empowers me to:

____

____

____

Day 4   My response to the question at the end of the devotion:

____

____

____

Day 5   Prayer:

____

____

____

~ Week 9 ~

"being confident of this, that he who began a good work in you will carry it on to completion until the day of Christ Jesus."
Philippians 1:6

Continuing with the situation mentioned from the previous week . . .

If your marriage partner professed a belief in Jesus in your early years together, but now says (s)he doesn't believe, you may find this disturbing and don't understand this change. Perhaps it is most discouraging because you would love to be able to experience the kind of oneness you two used to share in the Spirit.

Especially since most important in your life is your love relationship with Jesus. How sad you must be for this loss of sharing Christ with your spouse.

Pour out the sadness of your heart to God, even while taking heart in the promise of Philippians 1:6. Indeed, if your loved one at one time had accepted Jesus as Lord and Savior, then God will continue to work in her/his soul and spirit. If your special one's previous professed belief was not sincere and only surface level, then consider this a wonderful opportunity to intercede in her/his behalf.

God is patient, not wanting anyone to perish, but desiring that everyone come to repentance. (2 Peter 3:9) Since our Lord is patient, how can we be anything less?

When you tilt toward impatience, will you claim the promises of Philippians 1:6 and 2 Peter 3:9?

~ Week 9 Reflections ~

Day 1   This week's verse in full, or portion thereof:

____

____

____

Day 2   This verse is meaningful to me in that:

____

____

____

Day 3   This verse empowers me to:

____

____

____

Day 4   My response to the question at the end of the devotion:

____

____

____

Day 5   Prayer:

____

____

____

~ Week 10 ~

"Do not neglect your gift . . . . Be diligent in these matters; give yourself wholly to them, so that everyone may see your progress. Watch your life and doctrine closely. Persevere in them, because if you do, you will save both yourself and your hearers."

1 Timothy 4:14-16

God blessed Queen Esther with beauty and the courage to speak and act. At the potential cost of her life, she approached King Xerxes. To stand in the king's court without being summoned meant death if the king didn't hold out his gold scepter to enter his presence. Esther bravely petitioned the king to spare her life and her people—whose lives were on the brink of annihilation.

Esther embraced her gifts—beauty and courage—for such a time as this.

Centuries later, Paul, in his letter to Timothy captured the essence of Queen Esther's "giving herself wholly" to her gifts of beauty and courage. As she did so, she kept a close watch on herself by fasting. In the process, Esther saved herself and an entire nation of Jews.

How are you using your gift(s)? What are you doing to keep a close watch on yourself in order that you—through Christ—will save both yourself and your hearer?

~ Week 10 Reflections ~

Day 1   This week's verse in full, or portion thereof:

____

____

____

Day 2   This verse is meaningful to me in that:

____

____

____

Day 3   This verse empowers me to:

____

____

____

Day 4   My responses to the questions at the end of the devotion:

____

____

____

Day 5   Prayer:

____

____

____

~ **Week 11** ~

"There is a time for everything, and a season for every activity under the heavens:"

Ecclesiastes 3:1

In the seemingly hopeless situation of Jeremiah's courtyard confinement, God urged Jeremiah to call upon Him. Jeremiah 33:3 reveals God's promise if he did so.

The promise? "'Call to me and I will answer you and tell you great and unsearchable things you do not know.'"

Subsequently, God delivered a devastating report. Yikes!

But . . . then the Lord promised health, healing, peace and security. "'The days are coming,' declares the LORD, 'when I will fulfill the good promise I made to the people of Israel and Judah.'" (v.14)

God's timing and ways are perfect, so it's all about you trusting Him and His Word. The Holy Spirit will help as you continue to entrust your loved one to the Lord. Because as the above verse states, "For everything there is a season, and a time for every matter under heaven." In your situation—as in Jeremiah's—God's answer as you call upon Him may not initially be what you want to hear. Yet, in the end, God promises peace, regardless of what you presently see in the life of your loved one.

Trust in God is not based upon what you want Him to do, but upon His plan. When you accept this, peace ministers to you.

What can you do—as you wait for God's timing—to have the peace of His promise?

~ *Week 11 Reflections* ~

Day 1 This week's verse in full, or portion thereof:

____

____

____

Day 2 This verse is meaningful to me in that:

____

____

____

Day 3 This verse empowers me to:

____

____

____

Day 4 My response to the question at the end of the devotion:

____

____

____

Day 5 Prayer:

____

____

____

~ Week 12 ~

"if we are faithless, he remains faithful, for he cannot disown himself."
2 Timothy 2:13

You have been praying for your loved one's salvation and recently learned some exciting news. News that your special person professed faith in Christ at a church camp or revival meeting, or somewhere else as a child. And the friend sharing this information with you is convinced it was a true conversion. However, over the years your loved one veered off the path and no longer holds to her/his faith.

2 Timothy 2:13 is a promise from God you can hold onto. When your loved one accepted Jesus, at that moment, Christ came to live within her/him. Jesus cannot deny Himself; He must indeed be true to who He is. He is still alive within all those who ever invited Him into their hearts.

So, how do you now pray for that individual?

Perhaps: *Lord Jesus, I need to let go and let You do what You need to do in my loved one's life. My worry and fretting have only caused me distress, and have affected my witness to others. Help me trust in You and believe with all my soul and spirit that your Word is true. I want to hide this verse in my heart as an encouragement. Thank you for this promise and your faithfulness to me and my loved one.*

~ Week 12 Reflections ~

Day 1 **This week's verse in full, or portion thereof:**

____

____

____

Day 2 **This verse is meaningful to me in that:**

____

____

____

Day 3 **This verse empowers me to:**

____

____

____

Day 4 **My response to the question at the end of the devotion:**

____

____

____

Day 5 **Prayer:**

____

____

____

~ **Week 13** ~

"From heaven the LORD looks down and sees all mankind; from his dwelling place he watches all who live on earth—he who forms the hearts of all, who considers everything they do."
Psalm 33:13-15

Do you have more than one unsaved loved one for whom you are praying?

You can be assured that your loved ones' hearts are in God's hands. God knows exactly what is going on within them. The Lord is working to "fashion" or form each heart to draw all to Him.

In Psalm 139:1-4 we see that God knows us and our loved ones intimately. In a following verse, God says He has placed His hand on them. He knows what will come about every day of their lives, giving the promise that He is with them and will never leave them.

So, there is no need for you to worry about these precious people. Leave them in God's hands because He knows them far better than you do and loves them beyond however much you are capable of loving them. Yea and amen!

Know with all certainty that He is fashioning their hearts after His heart. What better design is there than this? What better place to be than in God's hands?

Close your eyes and envision handing your loved ones over to your Heavenly Father.

Now, how will you pray as you step away and leave them in your Heavenly Father's loving hands?

~ *Week 13 Reflections* ~

Day 1   **This week's verse in full, or portion thereof:**

____

____

____

Day 2   **This verse is meaningful to me in that:**

____

____

____

Day 3   **This verse empowers me to:**

____

____

____

Day 4   **My response to the question at the end of the devotion:**

____

____

____

Day 5   **Prayer:**

____

____

____

~ Week 14 ~

"'As the new heavens and the new earth that I make will endure before me,' declares the LORD, 'so will your name and descendants endure. From one New Moon to another and from one Sabbath to another, all mankind will come and bow down before me,' says the LORD."
Isaiah 66:23

God declared *all* flesh will worship Him. When the Lord says *all* He doesn't mean some. And when the Almighty makes a pronouncement it is done!

Taking in the context of when this verse was given, you may contend that God is speaking of the end of time, and you would be right. However, the point is, your loved ones will ultimately worship before God. Your prayers will make the difference between whether it is in the end times, or now when your loved ones worship the Lord.

Perhaps a moon-to-new-moon and Sabbath-to-Sabbath lack of evidence of your loved ones coming to the Lord keeps you from embracing God's vow in Isaiah. Or maybe even more than that it is the evidence of your loved ones staunchly holding an anti-God position that hinders your trust in God's promise.

When this is the case (your loved ones' resolute resistance), rejoice! Why would you do this? Because when a person steadfastly and persistently defies God, that is evidence of her or him being convicted. Yea and amen that God is working!

How does this vision of *all* peoples from all time—and for all time—encourage you to keep lifting your loved ones to our Heavenly Father?

~ Week 14 Reflections ~

Day 1   This week's verse in full, or portion thereof:

____

____

____

Day 2   This verse is meaningful to me in that:

____

____

____

Day 3   This verse empowers me to:

____

____

____

Day 4   My response to the question at the end of the devotion:

____

____

____

Day 5   Prayer:

____

____

____

~ Week 15 ~

"At one time we too were foolish, disobedient, deceived and enslaved by all kinds of passions and pleasures . . . But when the kindness and love of God our Savior appeared, he saved us, not because of righteous things we had done, but because of his mercy."
Titus 3:3-5

Is your loved one mired in a life of worldly pleasures? Does (s)he put her/his own passions first and foremost? If so, do you see these as impossible barriers to overcome as a lost cause?

Consider that perhaps your special person's lifestyle pales in comparison to that of Saul of Tarsus. Saul—later named Paul—actively gave his approval of killing followers of Christ (Acts 8:1); but that was before the Lord got Paul's attention. What a blessing it is to all of us all these centuries later that Paul turned away from his persecution of believers and became a believer himself. And went on to not only faithfully serve God in the face of his own persecution but to write letter after letter to early churches, which even now provide us with guidance, encouragement, enlightenment, and inspiration.

May Paul's testimony arm you with encouragement that your loved one is not a lost cause, that God can tap her/him on the shoulder in some fashion, and reveal His character to your dear one, and in doing so, call her/him into His presence.

How can show your special person you and the Lord love her/him regardless of her/his lifestyle?

~ *Week 15 Reflections* ~

Day 1   This week's verse in full, or portion thereof:

____

____

____

Day 2   This verse is meaningful to me in that:

____

____

____

Day 3   This verse empowers me to:

____

____

____

Day 4   My response to the question at the end of the devotion:

____

____

____

Day 5   Prayer:

____

____

____

~ Week 16 ~

"The Lord is not slow in keeping his promise, as some understand slowness. Instead he is patient with you, not wanting anyone to perish, but everyone to come to repentance."
2 Peter 3:9

It may seem as if you have been praying for your loved one's salvation forever. It might even appear that this wonderful event will never happen.

Does this press heavily on you day in and day out? Does it wear you down, so much so that you wonder if your time spent in prayer and in waiting are in vain?

Even so, you persist. You will not give up! Especially since you know full well that your timing is not God's. The verse above assures you the Lord is NOT slow about His promises. And He absolutely does not want anyone—which includes that special person in your life—to depart from this life without coming to Him and accepting His salvation. Yea and amen!

As you lift your loved one to God, of course you are eager for her/him to surrender to the Lord. When you see no movement in that direction, admit to your Heavenly Father your impatience, which is in part because you fear your beloved will pass away before accepting Christ.

Will you store 2 Peter 3:9 in your memory to embrace the truth of it in the midst of your impatience?

~ *Week 16 Reflections* ~

Day 1   This week's verse in full, or portion thereof:

____

____

____

Day 2   This verse is meaningful to me in that:

____

____

____

Day 3   This verse empowers me to:

____

____

____

Day 4   My response to the question at the end of the devotion:

____

____

____

Day 5   Prayer:

____

____

____

~ Week 17 ~

"For the word of God is alive and active. Sharper than any double-edged sword, it penetrates even to dividing soul and spirit, joints and marrow; it judges the thoughts and attitudes of the heart."

Hebrews 4:12

A great way to pray is to lift God's words back to Him, releasing the power of the sword of the Spirit for whom you love dearly.

Which verses will you brandish?

Consider adding the following to your arsenal, claiming the verses for your loved one, replacing her/his name on the lines as indicated below . . . .

John 3:17 ". . . For God did not send his Son into the world to condemn the world (______), but to save the world (______) through him."

Lamentations 3:22 "Because of the LORD's great love we (______ is) are not consumed, for his compassions never fail."

2 Thessalonians 3:5 "May the Lord direct your hearts (______'s heart) into God's love and Christ's perseverance."

Romans 8:38-39 "For I am convinced that neither death nor life, neither angels nor demons, neither the present nor the future, nor any powers, neither height nor depth, nor anything else in all creation, will be able to separate us (______) from the love of God that is in Christ Jesus our Lord."

Romans 5:6 "You see, at just the right time, when we were (_______ was) still powerless, Christ died for the ungodly (_______)."

Which sword of the Spirit will you wield this day, this week to align yourself with God's heart and will?

~ *Week 17 Reflections* ~

Day 1   This week's verse in full, or portion thereof:

____

____

____

Day 2   This verse is meaningful to me in that:

____

____

____

Day 3   This verse empowers me to:

____

____

____

Day 4   My response to the question at the end of the devotion:

____

____

____

Day 5   Prayer:

____

____

____

~ **Week 18** ~

***". . . I call as my heart grows faint; lead me to the rock that is
higher than I."***

Psalm 61:2

Does it feel as if you are between a "Rock and a Hard Place" when
it comes to unconditionally accepting your friend as (s)he is, when
you want her/him to change—to be saved?

If only . . . you think. Even if you try to hide your
disappointment or unacceptance of her/his beliefs (or lack of),
(s)he senses this. Likewise, you feel this barrier between you. Your
heart is overwhelmed because this is not what you want for either
of you. Yet there it is—conflicting and contradictory emotions.

Perhaps your friend called you on this when (s)he said, "It
seems as if you don't accept me as I am." Or in her/his honesty
said, "It feels like you are always judging me."

Where do you go from here, whether or not this is out in the
open?

Run, not walk, from this hard place to the rock that is higher
than you. God knows each of you intimately. He loves both of you
unconditionally. Nothing is too hard for Him. Nothing. Which
means He can fill you with unconditional love for your friend. You
need only ask Him for this gift to give her/him.

It will liberate both of you. You will be free of that barrier.
Your friend will be free from your expectations of her/him.

Now God can work!

Will you approach your Lord and Savior for His help in loving your friend unconditionally?

~ *Week 18 Reflections* ~

Day 1   This week's verse in full, or portion thereof:

____

____

____

Day 2   This verse is meaningful to me in that:

____

____

____

Day 3   This verse empowers me to:

____

____

____

Day 4   My response to the question at the end of the devotion:

____

____

____

Day 5   Prayer:

____

____

____

~ **Week 19** ~

"In the same way, the Spirit helps us in our weakness. We do not know what we ought to pray for, but the Spirit himself intercedes for us through wordless groans."
Romans 8:26

Do you struggle with the right words to share with your loved one?

Often when you are so overwhelmed or overwrought, you don't know what or how to pray, perhaps because you are focused on the storm around you.

Take heart . . . God has created a unique communication pathway through the Holy Spirit who came to live in you when you accepted Jesus as your Savior. (Acts 2:38)

Even in your confusion and difficulty knowing what to approach the Lord for, the Spirit steps in and bridges the gap in your behalf. Hallelujah!

As you go deeper into God's Word, growing in your faith and knowledge, you learn how to listen to and receive the Holy Spirit's counsel.

Just as God promised Moses in Exodus 4:11-12 that He would help Moses speak and would teach him what to say, so will the Lord bless you with effective speech.

Will you surrender even now to the Holy Spirit and allow Him to work within and through you as you pray for that special person in your life?

~ *Week 19 Reflections* ~

Day 1   This week's verse in full, or portion thereof:

____

____

____

Day 2   This verse is meaningful to me in that:

____

____

____

Day 3   This verse empowers me to:

____

____

____

Day 4   My response to the question at the end of the devotion:

____

____

____

Day 5   Prayer:

____

____

____

~ **Week 20** ~

"but those who hope in the LORD *will renew their strength. They will soar on wings like eagles; they will run and not grow weary, they will walk and not be faint."*
Isaiah 40:31

Does your loved one make hurtful comments about your faith?

David frequently encountered these situations and wrote, "My bones suffer mortal agony as my foes taunt me, saying to me all day long, 'Where is your God?' Why, my soul, are you downcast? Why so disturbed within me? Put your hope in God, for I will yet praise him, my Savior and my God." Psalm 42:10-11

Most likely your loved one is not your foe, but still may tease you about your belief in a God in whom (s)he doesn't believe. At times like this, you might find yourself as bone weary as David, and lacking strength. You need to rest your body, but more importantly you need to spiritually and emotionally rest in God's hands, putting your hope in Him—not in your own strength to save your loved one. For it is then that the Creator pulls you to Him and infuses you with His strength.

God's strength never fails you. It provides exactly what you need to take the next step, then another step on your journey of witnessing and praising Jesus, even when your path is littered with brambles—barbs tearing at your soul; or boulders—walls of resistance; or sinkholes—pits of hopelessness.

What do you see when you visualize God's strength within you?

~ Week 20 Reflections ~

Day 1   This week's verse in full, or portion thereof:

____

____

____

Day 2   This verse is meaningful to me in that:

____

____

____

Day 3   This verse empowers me to:

____

____

____

Day 4   My response to the question at the end of the devotion:

____

____

____

Day 5   Prayer:

____

____

____

~ Week 21 ~

"You should not gloat over your brother in the day of his misfortune . . . ."
Obadiah 1:12

As you have prayed for your biological brother, have you been patient with him? Has he been patient with you as you share your faith? Or have each of you become more entrenched in your respective stances?

If so, the enemy has had opportunity to whisper words of discouragement, disgust and damnation to both of you.

Have the following thoughts floated through your mind?

- *My brother is a fool to reject God.*
- *My brother deserves the consequences of his pridefulness.*
- *If only he would see how Jesus protects me, he wouldn't be so arrogant.*

These thoughts come in the form of "my" and "I" because Satan is a liar and a thief—a wolf in sheep's clothing. If he assaults you often enough with these thoughts, you eventually embrace them as your own. As you add your own judgments, you fuel the fire of the enemy. You will eventually be depleted emotionally, leading to discouragement, despair, and even worse, perhaps hatred. Which is where the enemy intends to take you. Thankfully, God reveals in Ephesians 6:12 this struggle is not against your brother but against the spiritual forces of evil. When you recognize this, you can resist the enemy's tactics to separate you from your loved one.

Then you can rebuke these thoughts in the name of Jesus and replace them with truth and insight from scripture.

How will you pray to take every thought captive to Christ (2 Corinthians 10:5)?

~ *Week 21 Reflections* ~

Day 1   This week's verse in full, or portion thereof:

____

____

____

Day 2   This verse is meaningful to me in that:

____

____

____

Day 3   This verse empowers me to:

____

____

____

Day 4   My response to the question at the end of the devotion:

____

____

____

Day 5   Prayer:

____

____

____

~ Week 22 ~

"I can do all things through him [Christ] who gives me strength."

Philippians 4:13

Chapter 30 of 1 Samuel tells of David's coming upon Ziklag only to find it destroyed and his two wives taken captive by the Amalekites. To add to that distress, David's own men threatened to kill him because their sons, daughters and wives had also been captured.

Does David give up, run away, or collapse under this weight? The Bible is clear on this— ". . . but David found strength in the LORD his God." (v.6)

Is it too big of a leap to see that your spouse/family member is temporarily held captive by the enemy?

Because your prayers have lifted this person into the hands of God, you *can* endure this situation, regardless of how long it takes— because you *can do all things through Christ who strengthens you.* Your sovereign Lord's power is far greater than that of the enemy and far greater than your loved one's resistance to God.

Even though your situation is not quite the same as David's, take encouragement and direction from David who inquired of the Lord, "Shall I pursue this raiding party? Will I overtake them?" To which the Lord directed him to pursue them, and told David he would overtake them and succeed in the rescue. (v.8)

How can you to continue to pursue your loved one in the way God would have you do?

~ Week 22 Reflections ~

Day 1 **This week's verse in full, or portion thereof:**

____

____

____

Day 2 **This verse is meaningful to me in that:**

____

____

____

Day 3 **This verse empowers me to:**

____

____

____

Day 4 **My response to the question at the end of the devotion:**

____

____

____

Day 5 **Prayer:**

____

____

____

~ Week 23 ~

*"Whoever is patient [slow to anger] has great understanding,
but one who is quick-tempered displays folly."*
Proverbs 14:29

Have you found yourself becoming angry at your loved one for failing to see the truth in God's Word? If so, remember that without revelation knowledge, you also were unable to see the truth. You can't make this happen for someone else. Rather than giving in to anger—which at its core is a feeling of helplessness—choose to relinquish your loved one to God.

Fear of the one you love spending eternity in the absence of God also has at its core a sense of helplessness. The reality is, you are powerless over others' lives as well as decisions they make. But you do possess the power of prayer!

Prayer changes situations, but just as importantly it changes you. When you let go of your loved one and leave her/him in God's hands, your anger and feeling of helplessness will dissipate. In this process, the Lord will bless you with great understanding.

If Satan can get you to nurse anger, he will succeed in chipping away at your relationship with your loved one and pull you away from Jesus. In fact, think back to the last time you were angry. Did you stew rather than draw near to Jesus or dive into the Bible?

Which will you choose . . . anger or understanding?

~ *Week 23 Reflections* ~

Day 1   This week's verse in full, or portion thereof:

____

____

____

Day 2   This verse is meaningful to me in that:

____

____

____

Day 3   This verse empowers me to:

____

____

____

Day 4   My response to the question at the end of the devotion:

____

____

____

Day 5   Prayer:

____

____

____

~ **Week 24** ~

"For the unbelieving husband has been sanctified through his wife, and the unbelieving wife has been sanctified through her believing husband. But if the unbeliever leaves, let it be so."
1 Corinthians 7:14

Are you doubtful about staying with an unbelieving spouse? Do you seriously consider leaving the marriage? Especially if (s)he mocks or criticizes you for your belief?

Or, have you considered, if only temporarily, how clash-free your life with your loved one would be if you abandoned your faith? Yet you know in your heart of hearts forsaking Jesus is not an option.

What if your spouse leaves you? You love her/him despite being unequally yoked, so do you quit praying for your beloved? Even then, how can you let go of the marriage?

Do you really want to give up on someone you love? The above verse does not speak to giving up; it only encourages you to let this person leave. God never gave up on you as promised in Jeremiah 31:3: "'. . . I have loved you with an everlasting love; I have drawn you with unfailing kindness.'" So how could you give up on someone you love, even though (s)he may not love you or the Lord?

Now more than ever, you need God's strength and loving arms to lift you up and carry you onward. This situation is not one He wants you to go alone.

What commitment to your marriage and the Lord will you make?

~ *Week 24 Reflections* ~

Day 1   This week's verse in full, or portion thereof:

____

____

____

Day 2   This verse is meaningful to me in that:

____

____

____

Day 3   This verse empowers me to:

____

____

____

Day 4   My response to the question at the end of the devotion:

____

____

____

Day 5   Prayer:

____

____

____

~ Week 25 ~

"A heart at peace gives life to the body, but envy rots the bones."
Proverbs 14:30

As you sit in the sanctuary, your eyes likely skim over the congregation of fellow believers and friends. Possibly your gaze rests upon couples. Do you envy your friends whose husbands worship with them?

Later, during the week, when your friends lovingly talk about their husbands who are saved, do you find yourself comparing that man to your unsaved betrothed?

Jealousy is one of Satan's effective tools for worming his way into your faith and emotional well-being. He will do anything to draw you away from the Lord and keep you from praying for your spouse. In fact, when Satan can accomplish this, he crosses the threshold not only into how you feel about yourself but also into how you feel about your husband. The enemy gets a double win when he can destroy your faith *and* your marriage.

When you feel envy rise within you, simply hold up the shield of faith against the evil arrows trying to penetrate your soul and spirit. Wield the sword of the Spirit to rebuke the enemy and pierce him with verse after verse. Rest assured this will render the devil ineffective in his cause. An added plus is the peace with which God will bless you.

Wouldn't you rather have peace than rotten bones?

How will you pray today and throughout the week?

~ *Week 25 Reflections* ~

Day 1   This week's verse in full, or portion thereof:

____

____

____

Day 2   This verse is meaningful to me in that:

____

____

____

Day 3   This verse empowers me to:

____

____

____

Day 4   My response to the question at the end of the devotion:

____

____

____

Day 5   Prayer:

____

____

____

~ **Week 26** ~

*"... If you remain in me and I in you, you will bear much fruit;
apart from me you can do nothing."*

John 15:5

Have you considered yourself a fruit bearer? If so, do you produce fruit of the Spirit? I.e. love, joy, peace, patience, kindness, goodness, faithfulness, gentleness, and self-control as mentioned in Galatians 5:22-23?

When you walk hand in hand with Jesus, these crops flourish. What a bounty you sow and harvest!

What does the Bible reveal regarding each of these?

Love—Is patient, kind and does not keep a record of wrongs. (1 Corinthians 13:4-5)

Joy—In His presence there is fullness of joy. (Psalm 16:11)

Peace—As you persistently trust in the Lord, He keeps you in perfect peace. (Isaiah 26:3)

Patience—Being patient brings you peace. (Proverbs 15:18)

Kindness—Kind words are sweet to the soul and healthy for the body. (Proverbs 16:24)

Goodness—Overcome evil with good. (Romans 12:21)

Faithfulness—God's faithfulness is your shield and fortress. (Psalm 91:4)

Gentleness—Your gentle answer turns away wrath. (Proverbs 15:1)

Self-control—The Holy Spirit gives you power, love, and self-discipline. (2 Timothy 1:7)

Which of these fruits will you cultivate today and this week as you interact with your loved one?

~ *Week 26 Reflections* ~

Day 1   This week's verse in full, or portion thereof:

____

____

____

Day 2   This verse is meaningful to me in that:

____

____

____

Day 3   This verse empowers me to:

____

____

____

Day 4   My response to the question at the end of the devotion:

____

____

____

Day 5   Prayer:

____

____

____

~ Week 27 ~

"This is the day which the LORD *hath made; we will rejoice and be glad in it."*
Psalm 118:24 (KJV)

There are days, and then there are days! Some start out sunny. Others dawn with threatening clouds.

However, the verse doesn't say that this is the *sunny* day the Lord has made. So regardless of what *kind* of day it is, rejoice and be glad in it. When you do, you establish an internal space that cannot be rained on.

What a powerful witness to your loved one! Even if you don't see how your attitude affects him or her, know that God is at work.

Such is the case with Ruth in the Old Testament. Her husband had just died and her mother-in-law, Naomi, told Ruth to leave. Ruth could have moped off in grief and bitterness. Instead, she looked past this dark day and into the future. She told Naomi she would go where she went, her people would be Ruth's people, and Naomi's God would be her God. Truly, this was the day the Lord had made, and Ruth was blessed because she embraced it.

Instead of looking at what you don't have—your loved one's salvation—embrace this day and rejoice in what the Lord has in store for your dear person.

What will your prayer include that will help you rejoice— even in the face of not knowing what the future holds?

~ *Week 27 Reflections* ~

Day 1   This week's verse in full, or portion thereof:

____

____

____

Day 2   This verse is meaningful to me in that:

____

____

____

Day 3   This verse empowers me to:

____

____

____

Day 4   My response to the question at the end of the devotion:

____

____

____

Day 5   Prayer:

____

____

____

~ **Week 28** ~

"Blessed [joyful] are those whose . . . hope is in the LORD *their God."*

Psalm 146:5

Do you hope this is the day your loved one will come to Christ? Yet, when evening dawns, (s)he continues to resolutely resist the Lord.

Will you let the fact that (s)he isn't saved get you down—robbing you of God's blessing of joy?

Often hope in others is misplaced. Indeed, in this case it is.

The enemy, which is not your loved one, wants to rob you of everything God has in store for you. However, the devil won't be able to take any of this from you when you put your hope and trust in the Lord.

Hannah (1 Samuel 1) asked God to look at her misery in barrenness and give her a boy. When Eli accused her of being drunk, she told him she was depressed and was simply pouring out her heart to the Lord, but continuing to hope in Him. Hope in the Lord's working carried her through and fired up hope for what God would do.

In this time of lack of evidence of your loved one's acceptance of Christ, pour out your heart to your Heavenly Father, always hoping in the midst of your angst or despondency. God promises that hope will bring you joy.

What do you need to relinquish to the Lord in order for your trust and hope in Him to be complete?

~ Week 28 Reflections ~

Day 1   This week's verse in full, or portion thereof:

____

____

____

Day 2   This verse is meaningful to me in that:

____

____

____

Day 3   This verse empowers me to:

____

____

____

Day 4   My response to the question at the end of the devotion:

____

____

____

Day 5   Prayer:

____

____

____

~ Week 29 ~

"Do not judge, or you too will be judged. For in the same way you judge others, you will be judged, and with the measure you use, it will be measured to you."

Matthew 7:1-2

As your loved one lives a moral and upright life, has (s)he expressed wanting his/her own supernatural experience of God, to the exclusion of church attendance and/or Bible study?

Do you see this as a "religion" for her/him and not a personal relationship with the Lord? Does this cause you concern and worry?

The good news is, it is not up to you to judge. That judgment belongs to God alone. What is up to you, is to continue to nourish your faith by drinking in God's Word, praising and worshipping Him, and demonstrating your love to this special person in your life.

Scripture demonstrates that God created us as unique individuals. There is nothing cookie-cutter about humans. Jeremiah 1:5 says, "Before I formed you in the womb I knew you, before you were born I set you apart;" Further on in Jeremiah 29, the Word says, "'For I know the plans I have for you', declares the LORD, 'plans to prosper you and not to harm you, plans to give you hope and a future.'"

Since God has a unique relationship with each of us, it stands to reason that each of us has a unique relationship with Him.

What will it take to trust God to fulfill the different and distinct plans He has designed for you *and* for your loved one?

~ Week 29 Reflections ~

Day 1   This week's verse in full, or portion thereof:

____

____

____

Day 2   This verse is meaningful to me in that:

____

____

____

Day 3   This verse empowers me to:

____

____

____

Day 4   My response to the question at the end of the devotion:

____

____

____

Day 5   Prayer:

____

____

____

~ **Week 30** ~

"Know that the LORD ***has set apart his faithful servant for himself; the*** LORD ***hears when I call to him."***
Psalm 4:3

You are set apart for God. Yea and amen! He does hear when you call to Him.

Yet it may not seem He has heard your pleas for your loved one's salvation, especially since there is not yet an indication of answered prayers. In fact, it may seem as if this special person in your life has drifted even further from the Lord.

You may wonder if you are the cause of this distancing, asking "Is it something I have done, or not done? Should I back off? Maybe I should just quit praying altogether."

When you admonish yourself in this way, you are assuming you have that much power over this person. The truth is, short of taking physical control, you cannot make anyone do anything, nor can you make anyone feel a certain way. These behaviors and feelings lie within the control and choices of that person.

So, how do you get *your* thoughts back on track? Romans 12:2 has the answer. ". . . be transformed by the renewing of your mind . . . ." You may struggle with this. Nonetheless, it is as simple as refusing to allow negative thoughts into your mind and replacing them with truth. This truth blossoms with each scripture verse you dwell on and store in your memory.

The Word is truly the sword of the Spirit, judging the thoughts and attitudes of the heart.

As you call to the Lord, what verse(s) will you claim to replace negative thoughts?

~ *Week 30 Reflections* ~

Day 1   This week's verse in full, or portion thereof:

____

____

____

Day 2   This verse is meaningful to me in that:

____

____

____

Day 3   This verse empowers me to:

____

____

____

Day 4   My response to the question at the end of the devotion:

____

____

____

Day 5   Prayer:

____

____

____

~ **Week 31** ~

"When your words came, I ate them. They were my joy and my heart's delight."
Jeremiah 15:16

Scripture presents several instances referring to the eating or devouring of God's words.

God instructed Ezekiel to eat the scroll He presented him. Ezekiel did and testified, ". . . So I ate it, and it tasted as sweet as honey in my mouth."—Ezekiel 3:3

A short time later, God said to him, "'Son of man, listen carefully and take to heart all the words I speak to you.'" (v.10)

This day are you ever so hungry for God's Word to bolster you, to lift you up?

Be encouraged by how Ezekiel was blessed by consuming God's words. Take into your heart all the Lord's words spoken to you through Bible verses and listen closely. For then you will be nourished and fortified to speak truths and endure amidst an unbeliever.

Even Job, in the midst of his trials, treasured the words of God more than his "daily bread." (Job 23:12) This speaks to the power and encouragement of God's Word, which is available to you!

Draw upon Jeremiah's, Ezekiel's, and Job's experiences to be blessed by God's love letters to you through His Word.

What other people in the Bible can you identify who embraced God's speaking into their lives and were strengthened and encouraged because of it?

~ Week 31 Reflections ~

Day 1   This week's verse in full, or portion thereof:

____

____

____

Day 2   This verse is meaningful to me in that:

____

____

____

Day 3   This verse empowers me to:

____

____

____

Day 4   My response to the question at the end of the devotion:

____

____

____

Day 5   Prayer:

____

____

____

~ Week 32 ~

"It's not important who does the planting, or who does the watering. What's important is that God makes the seed grow."
1 Corinthians 3:7 (NLT)

Are you in a season of drought in "seed planting" with your loved one?

In Genesis 26, Isaac was in the midst of a literal drought. What did he do? He obeyed the Lord to stay put and plant seeds. The Lord then blessed Isaac with crops beyond measure.

Is God calling you to stay put? To continue to till, to plant? If you obey His leading, God will do the watering, and you will reap a bountiful harvest. Your loved one *will* experience the fruit of your labors.

Imagine that glorious day! This is the vision God has for you and your loved one. Your Lord and Savior will indeed make the seed grow, as promised in 1 Corinthians 3:7.

Even at that, you may ask, "In what season do I sow?" "Do I throw out words, scattering seeds on untilled ground, hoping they will take root? Or do I wait for the right time to see the dirt softened, ready to receive seeds?"

Ask God to show you what, when, where, and how to plant. He will reveal all of this in your earnest seeking.

Whatever seeds you plant, God will make them sprout, and not only grow but flourish.

What seeds will you sow—seeds of truth? Seeds of encouragement? Seeds of awareness of God's infinite love for your special person?

~ *Week 32 Reflections* ~

Day 1   This week's verse in full, or portion thereof:

____

____

____

Day 2   This verse is meaningful to me in that:

____

____

____

Day 3   This verse empowers me to:

____

____

____

Day 4   My responses to the questions at the end of the devotion:

____

____

____

Day 5   Prayer:

____

____

____

~ **Week 33** ~

"Do not let your hearts be troubled. . . . My Father's house has many rooms; if that were not so, would I have told you that I am going there to prepare a place for you?"

John 14:1-2

Is your heart troubled today? The Bible reveals how often God's people experienced this state of being.

The Lord said to Joshua, "'Do not be afraid; do not be discouraged, for the LORD your God will be with you wherever you go.'"—Joshua 8:33

The Lord was sending Joshua across the Jordan River to a land God was giving the Israelites. He repeatedly told Joshua not to fear or be discouraged. But the stipulation was Joshua must be obedient and meditate on the Book of the Law.

When God puts conditions on something it is because He knows what we must do to stay on the right path.

When you first set out on your witness journey, did you imagine it would take this long? Do you wonder if your prayers will ever be answered? If you are discouraged, gird yourself with scripture. Just as God told Joshua to meditate on His Word so Joshua wouldn't be discouraged, know that encouragement is but a breath away for you as well.

Would you pray the following now to quiet your troubled heart?

Dear Lord, thank you that your house has many rooms and that you have gone there to prepare a place for me. Please work within my loved one so (s)he may also eternally inhabit one of these rooms. Thank you for anchoring me in your Word and easing my troubled heart.

~ Week 33 Reflections ~

Day 1   **This week's verse in full, or portion thereof:**

____

____

____

Day 2   **This verse is meaningful to me in that:**

____

____

____

Day 3   **This verse empowers me to:**

____

____

____

Day 4   **My response to the question at the end of the devotion:**

____

____

____

Day 5   **Prayer:**

____

____

____

~ **Week 34** ~

"Be joyful in hope, patient in affliction, faithful in prayer."
Romans 12:12

Previously, you read of hope. Weeks have passed, and perhaps you still haven't seen the fruit of your prayers.

Still, you persistently lift this special person in your life up to God and continue to hope for her/him to accept Jesus as Savior. Are you getting weary, your patience wearing thin? In the face of this weariness it is easy to lose hope, let alone be *joyful* in it.

Yet God has filled you with everything you need to have joy—the Holy Spirit, His Word, His love, His peace that passes all understanding (Philippians 4:7), and His promise to fill you with hope—"May the God of hope fill you with all joy and peace as you trust in Him, so that you may overflow with hope by the power of the Holy Spirit." (Romans 15:13)

Even as he was chained in prison, biblical Paul remained joyful. Can you think of anyone more patient than he was in his afflictions? And still he remained faithful in prayer. You see, Paul was not alone. The Holy Spirit was with Paul, in him, and filled the jail cell with His presence.

You don't have to drum up hope in your own strength. The Holy Spirit's power will do that for you, filling you with joy and peace in the bargain.

How have you acknowledged *and embraced* the Holy Spirit's presence within you?

~ *Week 34 Reflections* ~

Day 1   This week's verse in full, or portion thereof:

____

____

____

Day 2   This verse is meaningful to me in that:

____

____

____

Day 3   This verse empowers me to:

____

____

____

Day 4   My response to the question at the end of the devotion:

____

____

____

Day 5   Prayer:

____

____

____

~ Week 35 ~

"The LORD does whatever pleases him, in the heavens and on the earth, in the seas and all their depths."
Psalm 135:6

If God does whatever He wants, is it futile to pray for your loved one?

Although God's *character* never changes, He does give assurance in Hosea 11:8 that prayers reach Him and touch Him. He says, "My heart is changed within me, all my compassion is aroused."

There is a reason God doesn't answer every prayer just as you ask. If He did, wouldn't that make you all powerful? Think of how catastrophic it would be for you and the world if you were all powerful but not all-knowing and all-loving. If God were compelled to do everything you ask, what would be the difference between Him and you?

Thank the Lord that He is in control, that He knows what is best for you and your loved one, and that He loves you both enough to withhold or give as He sees fit.

What if this means you will not see your dear one come to the Lord in your lifetime? Can you accept this? If you knew this to be a fact, would you change the way you pray, or stop praying altogether?

Or would you intensify your pleas to your Father in Heaven and inundate your petitions with gratitude as well—thanking the Lord that He is in control, thanking Him that He does hear your prayers, and thanking Him that does know best?

How will you pray this moment and this week?

~ *Week 35 Reflections* ~

Day 1   This week's verse in full, or portion thereof:

____

____

____

Day 2   This verse is meaningful to me in that:

____

____

____

Day 3   This verse empowers me to:

____

____

____

Day 4   My response to the question at the end of the devotion:

____

____

____

Day 5   Prayer:

____

____

____

115

~ **Week 36** ~

"... 'Be still, and know that I am God;'"
Psalm 46:10

Translated from the Hebrew word *rapha*, to be still means to be weak, to let go, to release. At its core, it means surrender. Only when you surrender to Yahweh can you begin to know who He is.

When you read all of the 46th Psalm, you discover a glimpse of who God is. Your refuge and strength. An ever-present help in trouble. It is when you rest your spirit in His loving arms, that you *know* these attributes of the Lord.

Letting go of trying to "engineer" your loved one's acceptance of Christ leads to this stillness of which God speaks.

There is no greater place to be than in this sweet surrender—there is no greater peace, no greater joy, no greater serenity.

Have you completely surrendered, not just the fate of your loved one, but your will, your life—i.e. what may or may not happen—to God Almighty, your Maker, Creator of heaven and earth?

If so, then you know it is a daily surrender that draws you into His presence.

If you have never surrendered completely, and have difficulty doing this, starting with praise and worship is a wonderful and rewarding first step.

As you are still before God, how will you, at this moment, approach His throne of grace and mercy?

~ *Week 36 Reflections* ~

Day 1   This week's verse in full, or portion thereof:

____

____

____

Day 2   This verse is meaningful to me in that:

____

____

____

Day 3   This verse empowers me to:

____

____

____

Day 4   My response to the question at the end of the devotion:

____

____

____

Day 5   Prayer:

____

____

____

~ Week 37 ~

"Hope deferred makes the heart sick, but a longing fulfilled is a tree of life."
Proverbs 13:12

Waiting is hard on the nerves. Sometimes a lengthy wait for what you want so badly can affect you much like a lingering illness. This situation is what Solomon speaks to when he says, "Hope deferred makes the heart sick."

When something "makes the heart sick," despair, depression, and physical sickness can result. As your wait for your loved one to come to the Lord draws out year after year, your expectation can turn into hopelessness, which could lead you into a spiritually dry desert. It is in this place that you are most vulnerable to the enemy's attacks.

You need a pick-me-up. God offers just the remedy. (Actually, He offers lots.) Proverbs 17:22 states: "A cheerful heart is good medicine, but a crushed spirit dries up the bones."

How can you be cheerful when you are down in the molly grubs?

Try laughing even if you don't find anything funny. Your body doesn't know the difference between laughing from humor or laughing for health.

In his book, *Laughter in Hell, the Use of Humor During the Holocaust,* Steve Lipman cites Jews who used not only prayer but humor, revealing that humor proved to be their pleasant spice, spiritual resistance from oppression, and a currency of hope.

So, spice up your life with laughter to purchase hope and resist that which is oppressing you.

Taking a step of faith, what can you think of which is totally not funny but laugh anyway?

~ *Week 37 Reflections* ~

Day 1 This week's verse in full, or portion thereof:

____

____

____

Day 2 This verse is meaningful to me in that:

____

____

____

Day 3 This verse empowers me to:

____

____

____

Day 4 My response to the question at the end of the devotion:

____

____

____

Day 5 Prayer:

____

____

____

~ Week 38 ~

"It [love] always protects, always trusts, always hopes, always perseveres."
1 Corinthians 13:7

Because you love your friend or family member, you continue to trust, hope, and persevere in your faith that God hears your prayers for this person's salvation.

But what if your perseverance waivers? And you don't have the strength or endurance on this day to hold up and hold out for hope.

This is when it is vital to tap into God's love for you—and for your loved one—because you know for certain God's love is unfailing, as promised in Psalm 136:26. You are human, with human limitations and weaknesses. The Lord knows this about you, which is why He has packed promises in His Word.

Don't let guilt swoop in on you like a predator wanting to devour what little faith and hope you have at this moment. Call on God's love to protect you and that special person in your life. Ask the Lord to increase the measure of your trust, hope and perseverance.

Raise the sword of the Spirit; speak forth words from scripture to protect you from the enemy's bombardments of blame, shame, self-reproach, and condemnation—all thieves serving the enemy.

Which verse(s) will you brandish today and this week?

~ Week 38 Reflections ~

Day 1   This week's verse in full, or portion thereof:

____

____

____

Day 2   This verse is meaningful to me in that:

____

____

____

Day 3   This verse empowers me to:

____

____

____

Day 4   My response to the question at the end of the devotion:

____

____

____

Day 5   Prayer:

____

____

____

~ **Week 39** ~

"So Peter was kept in prison, but the church was earnestly praying to God for him."
Acts 12:5

Even when God answers the prayers of His children, it is not always recognized or believed.

Such was the case when Peter slept between two soldiers, bound with chains and with sentries guarding the prison. A short distance away, Peter's friends were fervently praying for him.

The result of their petitions to God?—"Suddenly an angel of the Lord appeared and a light shone in the cell. He struck Peter on the side and woke him up. 'Quick, get up!' he said, and the chains fell off Peter's wrists." (v.7)

Peter followed the angel out of the prison but didn't realize what was happening. Not until the angel left him in the street did Peter have no doubt God had sent His angel to rescue him. At once, Peter went to Mary's house. A servant, Rhoda, answered the knock on the door, then ran to tell the people praying that Peter was there. It took some time for them to believe her.

Did they not believe Rhoda because she was a servant? Or because they didn't believe God would answer their prayers in this way or at this time? God released Peter from chains, and can free your loved one from all that binds her or him as well.

What keeps you from believing that even now God is answering your prayers for your loved one in His way and in His time?

~ *Week 39 Reflections* ~

Day 1 This week's verse in full, or portion thereof:

____

____

____

Day 2 This verse is meaningful to me in that:

____

____

____

Day 3 This verse empowers me to:

____

____

____

Day 4 My response to the question at the end of the devotion:

____

____

____

Day 5 Prayer:

____

____

____

~ Week 40 ~

"For the Spirit God gave us does not make us timid [fearful] but gives us power, love and self-discipline."
2 Timothy 1:7

You previously read about not being able to make somebody change or do what you want them to. Have you struggled with this reality? If so, it is because you want what is best for that person. But do you see the futility in continuing to try to "make" your loved one come to the truth? Even God doesn't *make* us do anything. He shows us the best way, then waits patiently for us to "see the light."

Of course you put energy and effort into leading your husband/wife, or someone dear to you to the Lord, but are you then stepping back and letting go and letting God do His work in your loved one?

The above verse in 2 Timothy is a promise from God. He has given you a spirit of power, love, and self-control. In Matthew 18, Jesus says, "Whatever we bind on earth, will be bound in heaven and whatever we loose on earth will be loosed in heaven." Now that is power! As you "loose" God's love and His Word into your loved one's life, you can be sure it will in some way have effect.

Notice in 2 Timothy God speaks of power, love, and self-control *in the same breath*. As you practice self-control (letting go of trying to control what others accept—or not), you embrace the power and love of God.

How freeing is this? Describe what this freedom does for you.

~ *Week 40 Reflections* ~

Day 1   This week's verse in full, or portion thereof:

____

____

____

Day 2   This verse is meaningful to me in that:

____

____

____

Day 3   This verse empowers me to:

____

____

____

Day 4   My responses to the entreaties at the end of the devotion:

____

____

____

Day 5   Prayer:

____

____

____

~ **Week 41** ~

"... The prayer of a righteous person is powerful and effective."
James 5:16

2 Kings 6 tells of the king of Aram at war with Israel. Elisha, a devout man of God, warned the king of Israel repeatedly about the Arameans' plans of attack. When the king of Aram discovered where Elisha was, he sent troops to surround that city.

Elisha's servant was terrified at the sight of the enemy's numbers and cried out to Elisha who told him not to be afraid because there were more with them than there were on the enemy's side. Elisha prayed for the servant's eyes to be opened to see a greater number of their own horses and chariots of fire all around.

How powerful and effective were the prayers of this righteous man!

You are righteous because of Jesus' redemption; as such you can approach God with confidence. Ask Him to open your eyes to see what He is doing in the life of your loved one.

However, even if God chooses not to reveal His working in this situation at this time, take heart from Psalm 77 where Asaph wrote of God performing miracles, and His mighty arm redeeming His people. Asaph spoke of God's path through the sea, though His footprints were not seen.

If it seems you are drowning in a sea of hopelessness, ask the Lord to increase your belief that He is forging a path despite no evidence of His footprints.

What threatens your prayer life from being all it can be?

~ Week 41 Reflections ~

Day 1   This week's verse in full, or portion thereof:

____

____

____

Day 2   This verse is meaningful to me in that:

____

____

____

Day 3   This verse empowers me to:

____

____

____

Day 4   My response to the question at the end of the devotion:

____

____

____

Day 5   Prayer:

____

____

____

~ **Week 42** ~

"You make known to me the path of life; you will fill me with joy in your presence, with eternal pleasures at your right hand."

Psalm 16:11

To steal your joy and intimacy with God, the enemy taunts with evidence that your loved one isn't saved. Rebuke the devil and draw near to Jesus, who without reservation or limit, will fill you with joy. Embrace God's promise that eternal pleasures await you. Do not let the enemy rob you of this.

Psalm 13 reveals David had lost the sense of being in God's presence. This distance between David and his Creator, in the face of David's enemy's presence, caused him great inner turmoil. He cried, "How long, LORD? Will you forget me forever? How long will you hide your face from me? How long must I wrestle with my thoughts and day after day have sorrow in my heart?" (v.1-2)

If you find yourself in this desolate wasteland, know it is the enemy working to convince you that your loved one will never know Jesus, and that all your care, concern, and efforts are useless. In this process, the enemy bullies his way in between you and God, for if Satan can cause you to question the Lord's presence, or at worst, cause you to lose that connection with God, (even though the Lord never leaves you), then the father of lies rejoices in victory.

What can you do to remain on the path of life and experience God's presence in order to be more than a conqueror in Christ?

~ *Week 42 Reflections* ~

Day 1   This week's verse in full, or portion thereof:

____

____

____

Day 2   This verse is meaningful to me in that:

____

____

____

Day 3   This verse empowers me to:

____

____

____

Day 4   My response to the question at the end of the devotion:

____

____

____

Day 5   Prayer:

____

____

____

~ Week 43 ~

"And we know that in all things God works for the good of those who love him, who have been called according to his purpose."
Romans 8:28

This verse doesn't say in *some* things, but rather in *all* things God is working for you because you love Him and He has called you for His purpose.

In your case, does *all* things mean marriage to an unsaved husband? If so, this means God is working even now in this situation for your good. You may not see how, but that's because you don't see the whole picture. Perhaps tears cloud your vision.

Yet, consider that pain-induced tears can cleanse your eyes so you may see the sight and might of your Lord and Savior. Did you know God stores your tears in a vessel?

David recorded this truth in Psalm 56:8: "You yourself have . . . put my tears in Your bottle. Are they not in Your records?" (HCSB)

That said, you do not have to see with your eyes the Lord ever beside you leading the way. The truth of this is in Psalm 77:19: "Your path led through the sea, your way through the mighty waters, though your footprints were not seen."

When you rely on your spiritual eyes for knowledge of the truth, comfort and assurance are yours to embrace.

What footprint of God's can you recognize in your marriage to an unsaved spouse?

~ *Week 43 Reflections* ~

Day 1   This week's verse in full, or portion thereof:

____

____

____

Day 2   This verse is meaningful to me in that:

____

____

____

Day 3   This verse empowers me to:

____

____

____

Day 4   My response to the question at the end of the devotion:

____

____

____

Day 5   Prayer:

____

____

____

~ **Week 44** ~

***"In the same way, let your light shine before others, that they
may see your good deeds and glorify your Father in heaven."***
Matthew 5:16

What do you do when your spouse or friend asks you to cease
and desist sharing the Lord, Bible verses, and/or your faith?

Respect her/his wishes.

Still, that doesn't mean you must quit praying for her/him.
Your private communications with the Lord are between Him and
you. This is a special time to pour out your heart to your Heavenly
Father. Hold nothing back. God loves these moments—hours—of
intimacy with Him. Listen to Him. Hear His heart for you and for
your spouse, your child, or your friend.

Just as you attend to what your loving Heavenly Father
shares with you, so too pay attention to what your loved one
discloses—without censure or judgment. The more you lend this
person an ear, the more you can show your devotion to her/him.
Will this win her/him over? Will (s)he then want to hear what you
have to say about Jesus?

Maybe or maybe not. But it will draw the two of you closer
together. Especially as you are mindful to love unconditionally—
something difficult to do without God. So, you see, you are still
witnessing to your loved one, just not in a way of which (s)he is
aware.

When your light shines in your household, your Father in heaven is glorified. Yea and amen!

How can you let your light shine today, this week, this year?

~ Week 44 Reflections ~

Day 1 This week's verse in full, or portion thereof:

____

____

____

Day 2 This verse is meaningful to me in that:

____

____

____

Day 3 This verse empowers me to:

____

____

____

Day 4 My response to the question at the end of the devotion:

____

____

____

Day 5 Prayer:

____

____

____

~ **Week 45** ~

"You, LORD, keep my lamp burning; my God turns my darkness into light."
Psalm 18:28

What a wonderful reality and promise this is to lift you up and into God's presence in those moments when it seems your loved one will never come to Christ—when the enemy takes your mind to dark places.

It must have been a very dark dwelling space for Mary and Martha when their brother Lazarus died. Undoubtedly, they had offered up fervent prayers for his healing during his illness and had even sent for Jesus to come in person. Yet now Lazarus was departed from this world.

Why didn't God answer the women's prayers in the way they expected? Jesus purposely delayed returning to their home knowing Lazarus was near death. When Jesus did arrive, He raised Lazarus from the grave and gave him back to his grieving sisters.

Jesus asked them, "Did I not tell you that if you believed, you would see the glory of God?"—John 11:40

When God delays answering your prayers, you can be certain He has something even greater in store for you and your loved one—to witness the glory of God.

As the Lord keeps your lamp burning, has He not asked you to believe He will turn your darkness into light—even as it appears your loved one is at present dead to Christ?

~ *Week 45 Reflections* ~

Day 1   This week's verse in full, or portion thereof:

____

____

____

Day 2   This verse is meaningful to me in that:

____

____

____

Day 3   This verse empowers me to:

____

____

____

Day 4   My response to the question at the end of the devotion:

____

____

____

Day 5   Prayer:

____

____

____

~ **Week 46** ~

"I keep my eyes always on the LORD. With him at my right hand, I will not be shaken."
Psalm 16:8

This verse calls you to keep your eyes on the Lord, so that when your gaze is fixed upon God, you will not be focusing on your loved one's lack of surrender to Christ, or on the discouragement that can foster.

When you look at God, what do you see? Close your eyes and imagine you are before Him. Ask Him to reveal more of His character to you. Wait for the Lord to do this.

Linger in His presence. Don't rush past what your Heavenly Father wants to show you. Allow Him to draw you close. Drink in the fragrance of His presence, the peace of His Being, the joy of His company.

Be still and know that He is God.

Know that He is Love. Know that He is Truth. Know that He is Life.

When you know these things, you will not be shaken!

David was in this place of confidence, even in the midst of his troubles. He wrote in Psalms 16:11: "You make known to me the path of life; you will fill me with joy in your presence, with eternal pleasures at your right hand."

What eternal pleasures come to your mind's eye when it is focused on the Lord?

~ Week 46 Reflections ~

Day 1   This week's verse in full, or portion thereof:

____

____

____

Day 2   This verse is meaningful to me in that:

____

____

____

Day 3   This verse empowers me to:

____

____

____

Day 4   My response to the question at the end of the devotion:

____

____

____

Day 5   Prayer:

____

____

____

~ **Week 47** ~

"... those who seek the LORD *lack no good thing."*
Psalm 34:10

Cling to this promise, for the wisdom in its counsel will buoy and sustain you when you feel pulled under.

As a shepherd boy, in his service to the king, and later as king himself, David encountered a multitude of difficult situations when he needed a counselor. Psalm after psalm reveals how he poured out his heart in both anguish and praise to God. In short, David knew where to turn for guidance, especially regarding relationships with those he loved. Having hidden God's Word in his heart, David called upon it and the Lord anytime and anywhere. (Fleeing for his life. Hiding in a cave. Etc.)

In God's Word, you, too, have this invaluable, ever-available Counselor—who will never lead you astray. Memorizing scripture verses allows access to counseling at your beckoning.

"Your statutes are my delight; they are my counselors."—Psalm 119:24

What a promise in days of darkness and nights of distress!

As you tuck God's Word into your memory, you are armed to praise His Holy name for teaching you life-giving decrees. As you seek your Heavenly Father's counsel, you will indeed be reminded that you lack no good thing.

What good things from the Lord come to mind even now as you memorize Psalm 34:10 and Psalm 119:27?

~ *Week 47 Reflections* ~

Day 1 This week's verse in full, or portion thereof:

____

____

____

Day 2 This verse is meaningful to me in that:

____

____

____

Day 3 This verse empowers me to:

____

____

____

Day 4 My response to the question at the end of the devotion:

____

____

____

Day 5 Prayer:

____

____

____

~ Week 48 ~

"You will keep in perfect peace those whose minds are steadfast, because they trust in you."
Isaiah 26:3

God's peace isn't defined by your circumstances but rather by His presence.

Moses knew he was in God's presence as he led the Israelites in flight from the Egyptians. He counted on God to deliver his people from captivity. Yet when the Israelites came to the Red Sea, the escape looked impossible with the vast body of water ahead and the advancing Egyptian army in the rear. The Israelites must have felt doomed, without hope, and completely devoid of peace at that moment. In fact, Exodus 14 tells us they were terrified and cried out to the Lord. They accused Moses of bringing them out of Egypt into the desert to die. Moses told his people to stand firm, that the Lord would bring deliverance. But God told Moses to move on.

Why didn't Moses implore God to part the waters? Perhaps he didn't know this was possible with God.

Do your prayers limit God as to how He can answer your prayers to save your loved one? Do you lack peace over this?

God's peace isn't an absence of conflict, but rather an incredible sanctuary—a peace that transcends all understanding, one that guards your heart and mind in the midst of what appears to be a Red-Sea-advancing-enemy impenetrable circumstance.

What can you do to let go of thoughts on how God will answer your prayers?

~ Week 48 Reflections ~

Day 1   This week's verse in full, or portion thereof:

____

____

____

Day 2   This verse is meaningful to me in that:

____

____

____

Day 3   This verse empowers me to:

____

____

____

Day 4   My response to the question at the end of the devotion:

____

____

____

Day 5   Prayer:

____

____

____

~ **Week 49** ~

"My God sent his angel, and he shut the mouths of the lions. They have not hurt me, because I was found innocent in his sight."
Daniel 6:22

"The atmosphere of expectancy is the breeding ground of miracles." This quote from Rod Parsley couldn't describe Daniel's faith any better.

We know from Scripture Daniel was a praying man. In fact, that's what got him into trouble. Despite the king's edict against prayer, Daniel prayed three times a day. Consequently, the king tossed him into the lions' den.

Now, because Daniel was a fervent prayer, doesn't it stand to reason that prior to being tossed into a den of death, he would have prayed for God to not let that happen? Yet, it did, and God answered Daniel's prayers for deliverance in a different way. All along Daniel expected God to save him. And because Daniel came out unscathed, King Darius decreed that people throughout his kingdom must fear and reverence the living God of Daniel.

God is the same yesterday, today, and forever and honors your faith in the same way as He did Daniel's trust in Him.

God is the Creator, the One who designs the Master Plan in His time and in His way.

What is it that impedes your capacity to believe God can or will answer your prayers in a manner which is way out of the box of your thinking?

~ Week 49 Reflections ~

Day 1   This week's verse in full, or portion thereof:

____

____

____

Day 2   This verse is meaningful to me in that:

____

____

____

Day 3   This verse empowers me to:

____

____

____

Day 4   My response to the question at the end of the devotion:

____

____

____

Day 5   Prayer:

____

____

____

~ Week 50 ~

"Do not be anxious about anything, but in every situation, by prayer and petition, with thanksgiving, present your requests to God. And the peace of God, which transcends all understanding, will guard your hearts and your minds in Christ Jesus."

Philippians 4:6

Are you anxious about your loved one's spiritual condition?

Take heart, for prayer changes things . . . and it changes you. As you draw near to God in supplication, your anxiety lessens because your anxious thoughts cannot occupy this space when you are in the caring arms of Christ.

When you hear the admonition to not be anxious about anything, you might think, *Easier said than done.* And you would be right. To simply will yourself not to be anxious doesn't work. It is as effective as wishing something not to happen.

Thank heavens, this verse in Philippians outlines distinct steps to release you from the clutches of anxiety.

Step 1: Draw near to your Heavenly Father.

Step 2: Open your heart to Him.

Step 3: Thank the Lord for this situation, as it births this opportunity to come to Him.

Step 4: Present your requests to the Lord.

Step 5: Listen to God's response.

Step 6: Receive the peace He promises.

These steps take practice and repeating, for you are a work in progress—as is your loved one when you leave her/him in Jesus' care.

How can you work these steps into your daily routine?

~ Week 50 Reflections ~

Day 1   This week's verse in full, or portion thereof:

____

____

____

Day 2   This verse is meaningful to me in that:

____

____

____

Day 3   This verse empowers me to:

____

____

____

Day 4   My response to the question at the end of the devotion:

____

____

____

Day 5   Prayer:

____

____

____

~ Week 51 ~

"... 'I have made you a light for the Gentiles, that you may bring salvation to the ends of the earth.'"
Acts 13:47

God chose Moses to lead the Israelites out of Egypt. Because of his speech impediment, Moses wasn't sure he was the right "light" to shine for this job. So God sent Aaron to help Moses speak. Still, the task must have felt overwhelming. Especially amid the attitude of the people murmuring about the not-so-cushy conditions while wondering around in the desert for forty years. Unfortunately, the Israelites missed the miracles right before their eyes day after day. They always had food, although it might not have been the filet mignon or Caesar salad they would have preferred.

God spoke to Moses, pointing out things the people had overlooked in their wanderings. "Your clothes did not wear out and your feet did not swell during these forty years." (Deuteronomy 8:4)

As you have shone your light, is it possible you have missed miracles God has performed, or if you did see them, have you forgotten them because your loved one hasn't made that final declaration of faith?

Ask God to open your eyes to recognize His hand at work in your life and in the life of your loved one. Ask Him to point out what you take for granted.

What do you see?

~ *Week 51 Reflections* ~

Day 1 **This week's verse in full, or portion thereof:**

____

____

____

Day 2 **This verse is meaningful to me in that:**

____

____

____

Day 3 **This verse empowers me to:**

____

____

____

Day 4 **My response to the question at the end of the devotion:**

____

____

____

Day 5 **Prayer:**

____

____

____

~ **Week 52** ~

"Not to us, O LORD, not to us but to your name be the glory,
because of your love and faithfulness."
Psalm 115:1

When that special person in your life accepts Jesus as Lord and Savior and begins an intimate relationship with Him, God's name will be glorified—fruit of His love and faithfulness to your loved one.

How you will revel jubilantly in this fruit produced from your love and faithfulness to the Sovereign Lord and to your friend, family member, or for whoever you ardently prayed!

Hallelujah!

Oh, for the glory of that day! Not only on earth but in heaven as well as angels join in the rejoicing!

Have you ever wondered how angels rejoice? Luke 2:13-14, Luke 15:7-10, Job 38:7, Psalm 148:2, and Revelation 5:11-13 all reveal a glimpse of what this looks like. What a celebration this must be with trumpets blowing and music filling the atmosphere with songs and shouts of praise and worship, joy permeating every fiber of every being.

Yea and amen!

How will you rejoice when your beloved invites Jesus into
her/his heart and life?

~ Week 52 Reflections ~

Day 1   This week's verse in full, or portion thereof:

____

____

____

Day 2   This verse is meaningful to me in that:

____

____

____

Day 3   This verse empowers me to:

____

____

____

Day 4   My response to the question at the end of the devotion:

____

____

____

Day 5   Prayer:

____

____

____

"... For the LORD your God will bless you in all your harvest and in all the work of your hands, and your joy will be complete."
Deuteronomy 16:15

Answers to Prayers

About the Author

Mary Stone, a follower of Christ and lover of God's Word, is devoted to sharing the wisdom and encouragement she has gleaned over the many years she has studied the Bible and worked in the field of Counseling. Her mission is threefold: for God to get the glory, for readers to get victory, and for Satan to be defeated.

Mary is an inspiring keynote speaker and author, who writes with openness and sincerity. She began her career in higher education after earning a Master's Degree in Counseling at the University of Nebraska, Kearney.

Lower Columbia College in Longview, Washington conferred upon her Faculty Emeritus for her years of outstanding and dedicated service in teaching and counseling. In addition to her career as a college Counselor, Mary practiced as a Licensed Mental Health Therapist for many years.

The author's first published non-fiction book, *Run in the Path of Peace—the Secret of Being Content No Matter What*, continues to garner her speaking engagements at women's conferences, book groups, and virtual conversations.

Mary loves to write, garden, travel, do puzzles, and spend time with her family—not necessarily in that order, depending on the day and on the Pacific Northwest weather.

She and her husband make their home in Washington state.

Mary invites you to contact her at:

maryellenstone@hotmail.com

and/or subscribe to her monthly devotional blog, *Sowing Seeds*, at:

https://marystonewriter.com

www.ingramcontent.com/pod-product-compliance
Lightning Source LLC
Chambersburg PA
CBHW071744150726

47998CB00005B/1790